.... WHAT'S AT ISSUE? ....

RELATIONSHIPS

Katrina Dunbar

www.heinemann.co.uk
Visit our website to find out more information about **Heinemann Library** books.

To order:
 Phone 44 (0) 1865 888066
 Send a fax to 44 (0) 1865 314091
🖳 Visit the Heinemann Bookshop at www.heinemann.co.uk to browse our catalogue and order online.

First published in Great Britain by Heinemann Library, Halley Court, Jordan Hill, Oxford OX2 8EJ, a division of Reed Educational and Professional Publishing Ltd. Heinemann is a registered trademark of Reed Educational & Professional Publishing Limited.

OXFORD MELBOURNE AUCKLAND JOHANNESBURG BLANTYRE
GABORONE IBADAN PORTSMOUTH NH (USA) CHICAGO

Designed by Tinstar Design (www.tinstar.co.uk)
Illustrations by Virginia Gray
Originated by Ambassador Litho Ltd
Printed in Hong Kong/China

04 03 02 01 00
10 9 8 7 6 5 4 3 2 1

ISBN 0 431 03544 X

British Library Cataloguing in Publication Data
Dunbar, Katrina
    Relationships. – (What's at issue?)
    1. Interpersonal relations – Juvenile literature
    I. Title
    302

Acknowledgements
The Publishers would like to thank the following for permission to reproduce photographs:
Bubbles: Pauline Cutler p43, Amanda Knapp p26, Frans Rombout p28, Jennie Woodcock pp5, 24, 33; Trevor Clifford Photography: pp11, 20, 34, 41; Sally and Richard Greenhill Photo Library: pp12, 22, 30, 39; Kobal Collection: p40; The Stock Market: Paul Barton p21, Charles Gupton p25, Mugshots p7, Jose Pelaez p13; Tony Stone Images: Penny Tweedie pp4, 8, 14, 37, Ziggy Kaluzny p18, Laurence Monneret p32.
Cover photographs by Bubbles: Frans Rombout

Our thanks to Julie Turner (School Counsellor, Banbury School, Oxfordshire) for her comments in the preparation of this book.

Every effort has been made to contact copyright holders of any material reproduced in this book. Any omissions will be rectified in subsequent printings if notice is given to the Publisher.

Any words appearing in the text in bold, **like this**, are explained in the Glossary.

Contents

Introduction

We call the bond we form with people we meet a relationship. There are many different kinds of relationships. We have distant or temporary relationships, such as with **acquaintances**, and formal relationships based on somebody providing a **professional** service to us, such as our doctors or teachers. Our close relationships are with our family, friends and people we are romantically involved with.

This book concentrates on relationships outside of the family, especially friendships and romantic relationships. It aims to help you to understand different kinds of relationships and to give more to, and get more from, the people in your life. It also looks at how your relationship with yourself – the way you feel about yourself – plays a huge part in the way you relate to others and the world around you. Strong, nurturing relationships help to create a healthy **society** for everybody.

Everybody needs friends

Relationships have inspired novels, poetry, films, songs and television more than any other subject. This is because they involve strong feelings, are central to human beings' lives, and underpin **society**. People of all ages spend hours talking and thinking about why they and others behave the way they do around each other. Take time one day to listen to what other people around you are talking about, whether it is on your way to school, in your home or amongst your friends. What proportion of the conversation is about relationships?

Having solid friendships makes a big difference in how confident and content most people feel in themselves.

Human nature

Most people are **sociable** by nature, and building good relationships with people they like makes them feel well-rounded and gives them a feeling of belonging. How successful they are at forming good relationships, and how important they feel to other people, makes a big difference to how good they feel about themselves.

Friendship

You can make friends with people of any age. Friends provide company when you want to have fun or to learn something new; they are people to share life's ups and downs with and to stop you feeling lonely; they are people to confide your deepest secrets to and to talk through your problems with. Friendship involves both the giving and taking of **respect**, trust and love.

As a teenager, you may feel that the only people who really understand you well are people of your own age. This makes friendships particularly important at this stage of life.

Having friends is particularly important as a teenager, because you may feel that your family does not understand you or your problems, and this is the time when you are learning to be independent from your family. Friendships with people of your own age may feel like your strongest relationships at this age, because your **peers** are going through the same stage in life and sharing a lot of the same experiences as yourself. If you feel lonely and have few friends, remember that there are lots of opportunities to make new friends, such as joining clubs, and it is more rewarding to have fewer good relationships than lots of **acquaintances**.

THE THREE KEYS TO GOOD RELATIONSHIPS

- Acceptance – we need to feel accepted for who we are, and to accept others.

- Understanding – we need to be understood, and to understand others.

- Communication – we need to be able to communicate what we are thinking and feeling through words, but also through our facial expressions and **body language**. We also need to listen to what others are communicating and watch their actions. This can be difficult, but it is important.

FACTS

In a survey of children aged 8–15:
- *99% declared relationships with people of their own age were important*
- *61% spent time with their friends every day or most days*
- *68% (over 2/3) felt they had a lot of friends*
- *44% (2/5) of 12–15 year-olds said they would talk to their friends about problems at home, compared with 24% who would talk to their mother and 12% to their father*
- *39% of the children, when asked what made them happy, gave responses that included having friends, doing things with friends or going out with friends*
- *girls' comments on their peer relationships showed more 'supportive' relationships than boys*
- *78% of girls said they had special friends, compared with 59% of boys*
- *80% of girls compared with 49% of boys said that they could always find a friend to talk to if they were upset*

NSPCC survey of UK children, 1996

Are you a good mate?

It is not easy to be a good friend. It is a real challenge to stay loyal, to make time for somebody else through thick and thin, and to behave decently at all times. None of us is perfect, and we all make mistakes, but do you pass the basic friendship test?

Whose side are you on?

'With friends like you, who needs enemies?'

'Perhaps you are perfect!'

① When your best mate turns up at a party, looking like a fashion victim:
You have a good laugh behind his or her back. Loyalty is less important than acting cool.

or

You don't ruin his or her good time at the party by saying anything, but the next time you are together, you start a conversation about 'looks' and the importance of finding your own style. Maybe you mention clothes of theirs that particularly suit them.

② When your friend lets you down at the last minute, for a Saturday night out that you've planned for ages, with no decent excuse:
You are furious. You do not say anything at the time, but you ignore your friend at school or make a few snide remarks to get your revenge.

or

You are honest. You tell them directly that you feel let down and angry. You ask how they would feel if you treated them like that, and ask them to promise not to do it again. Then you put it behind you and 'forgive and forget'. (If it does happen again, you reconsider whether they are worth having as a friend).

③ When your best friend's parents have suddenly become very strict, and all he or she talks about is how awful home life is:
You make it clear that he or she is becoming a bit of a pain, and should try to talk about something else. You spend as little time alone with him or her as possible.

or

You find it difficult that he or she is not much fun to be with, but you give up lots of time to listen and talk it through. You encourage him or her to join in with fun activities together with other friends, so that you both get a break from talking about problems. Suggest some activities that your friend's parents will approve of, so that their home situation might improve.

TIPS TO BECOMING A BETTER FRIEND

- Practise listening well – try not to interrupt or finish sentences for the other person. Notice how rare it is for people of any age to be good listeners.

- Try to be honest. This is difficult if you risk hurting your friend, making them angry, or being rejected (see no. 2 in the quiz).

- **Respect** your friend's right to have a private life and be their own person – it takes a lot of practice to find the right balance between being attentive to somebody and giving them **personal space**.

Think about a recent situation in which you feel you could have been a better friend. What might you do differently now?

You can tell that your friendship is a good one if you can talk honestly about your feelings, as well as do fun things together and have a laugh.

FACT

- *90% of young people said they could tell if their friend was worried about something, even if they had not said anything.*

  survey by the helpline charity
  Childline

Friends are equals

We have already looked at how difficult it can be to put good intentions about friendship into practice. Your friends probably do things that make you feel irritated, embarrassed, or plain bored at times. There are going to be days when you cannot listen to somebody else's problems because you feel overwhelmed by your own. Being a good friend does not mean always putting yourself second. The best friendships have a strong sense of **equality**, where both people listen to each other, want to spend the same amount of time together, and feel the same way about each other emotionally.

Can you keep a secret?

An important part of friendship is trust. As well as trusting each other not to judge too quickly, and **respecting** each other's opinions, friends need to be able to trust each other to keep information **confidential**. If you do not feel that you can tell your friend something and trust them to keep it to themselves if you ask them to, how likely are you to confide in them if you need to talk through something very personal that is bothering you?

Sometimes it feels very difficult to keep somebody else's secret. Maybe another good friend of yours suspects that you know something that they have not been told, and tries to persuade you to 'spill the beans'. You may not feel that the secret is a big deal, but what is important is how big a deal the secret is to the person who told you. It is up to them to decide who they trust with their secret, not you. Do you agree? If you do tell, the short-lived feeling of power when you reveal a juicy bit of gossip is soon wiped out by the guilt of betrayal, and fear of being found out as somebody who is a lousy friend.

Secrets which should not be kept

Are there any times when it is acceptable to break a friend's confidentiality? A true friend tries to act for the best for their friends. There may be times when it is important to seek help for a friend who has a problem which is too big to solve on their own or which is going to get worse if it remains a secret; for example addiction to drugs or alcohol.

The best way to make sure that you keep your friend's trust is to tell them how worried about them you are, and to try to persuade them to seek help for themselves. You can be there to support them through the feelings of fear or shame they may have about doing this.

If you are not sure what to do, talk to a responsible adult. Alternatively, you could

One way to test the strength of a friendship is to ask yourself whether you would trust that friend to keep a secret.

CASE STUDY

This is Jane's story about what happened when she didn't keep her best friend's secret.

'My best friend Mette came into school last week, sobbing. She told me during break that her older brother had been arrested for helping steal a car. He was at this school until last year, and used to be a bit of a heart throb.

'Of course, everyone else had noticed how upset Mette was, and another friend of both of ours took me aside later to ask if I knew what was up. I couldn't resist telling her, but I thought I could trust her not to tell anyone else. It was only when I got to school the next morning and a girl who doesn't like either Mette or me said: "Have you heard the latest about Mette's brother?" that I realized what I had done by turning Mette's personal nightmare into gossip.

'Mette will not speak to me now, and I feel terrible about letting her down so badly just when she needed a good friend she could trust.'

telephone a helpline like Childline (see page 46 for details). You can talk in confidence to these kinds of helplines, and discuss whether you should keep your friend's secret, without giving either your or your friend's names.

If your friend flatly refuses to seek help, or to give you permission to seek help on their behalf, you may have to risk losing the friendship rather than watch them go under because of a serious problem in their life that they need **professional** help with. This is a tough choice to have to make, but is minding your own business being a true friend?

9

When the going gets tough

It is normal to have problems

As we develop into adults, our bodies undergo lots of physical changes, known as **puberty**, and we have very strong feelings. Being a teenager can feel like riding a rollercoaster as our moods change. Problems which seem the end of the world one day, such as a bad mark for an essay or failing to get into a sports team, turn out to be completely unimportant the next day. One of the biggest challenges for human beings, at whatever age, is learning to accept that everyday life is full of ups and downs.

When is it serious?

Nobody is free of worries all of the time. But problems can range from the trivial, such as your favourite t-shirt being in the wash when you want it, to serious issues that stop people enjoying life. It is important to recognize the difference between the two. The best way to judge the seriousness of a problem is by checking how much it is on your mind and upsetting you, and if it feels like a continuing worry rather than something that will quickly pass. If a friend talks about a problem a lot, or often seems distracted, that is a sign that there may be something seriously wrong that they need help with.

FACT

Problems, like eating disorders, often start as a response to other problems such as family unhappiness or school pressures.

THE TWO MAIN KINDS OF PROBLEMS

1. Those caused by things other people are doing, and are outside the control of the person with the problem. These are problems like bullying or **racism**, emotional neglect and **sexual or physical abuse**. People who pick on other people often rely on their victims being too scared to take action.

2. Those that only involve the person with the problem. These are problems such as eating disorders, for example anorexia nervosa – where a person avoids eating and loses a lot of weight – or getting very stressed about pressures of school work, or getting depressed about family problems such as violence at home or divorce.

Whatever the situation, sensible action to tackle the problem is always the best way forward. Serious problems rarely go away by themselves, and may only get worse if ignored.

Talking always helps

There is a saying that 'a problem shared is a problem halved', and it is amazing how often just the act of telling somebody else about it can reduce a problem's importance instantly. This is because explaining it aloud helps you to feel more distant and objective about it, and to put it in **perspective**.

Talking to somebody else about something that is bothering you can help you think about it more clearly. Do you talk about things that worry you, or keep them bottled up?

TAKING ACTION

Here is a list that you can use for yourself, or to help a friend. If it is a friend you are worried about, encourage them to go with you to seek help if possible.

1. Admit to yourself that this problem has got too big for you to sort out yourself, and that you need some help. This may be from a **professional counsellor,** if you are abusing yourself in some way or deeply distressed by family events, for example.

2. Keep a record of what is happening, such as a diary of events.

3. As soon as you become aware that something is bothering you, talk to somebody you trust about it; this may be a teacher, a school counsellor, or another reliable adult. There are many helplines and charities which offer help to any young person with a problem. Two of the best known are Childline and NSPCC (see pages 46–7 for details). If you do not feel that you are getting the support you need from the first person you talk to, then try somebody else. Do not give up.

Do you want to be in my gang?

It is natural for most teenagers to want to be part of a group or gang.

Choosing your own family

So much is changing for you as you are beginning to explore who you want to be as an independent adult, rather than as your parents' child. Finding a group who you feel comfortable with can feel like creating an alternative family of your own choice. Unlike your natural family, or your carers if you live in a **foster family** or **care home**, the members of your gang have the same ideas as you, enjoy the same activities, and speak the same language. You can sometimes feel as if your parents or the people who are looking after you do not understand anything about you – it can be very hard work. Do you ever feel like this?

The up side

At its best, being part of a group can give you a feeling of belonging, and build your self-confidence. Spending most of

Being part of a group or gang has its ups and downs – have fun, but make sure you don't end up completely changing your own views and personality to fit with the 'in' crowd.

your time with just one best friend can feel smothering, but within a group there are a variety of characters to give you plenty of entertainment.

Social activities can be more fun in a group. Most importantly, you always have other people to spend break times at school with and you never have to spend time on your own unless you want to.

The down side

If you watch wildlife programmes on television, you will probably have noticed that in rigid animal 'gangs', such as herds or packs, there is always a leader and usually one animal identified as the weakest member. Human gangs follow the same pattern, even if none of the members state openly who the leader is, or if the leadership **role** shifts between members from time to time. In addition, each member may have a clear role according to their personality – you might be the one that makes everybody else laugh, the daring one or the one who is always late. But, having a role within a gang can hold you back from bringing your whole self to the group. If your role is a negative one, it can give you a damaging view of yourself.

The scapegoat

In every gang there comes a time when one person within it becomes a target for members to take out their frustrations on. This is the role of the scapegoat, and he or she may eventually leave the gang because they feel so bullied, or be pushed out of it. Having your entire gang turn on you can feel like the end of the world, and you may never even know why it has happened. Sadly, scapegoating is one of the ways that humans try to make themselves feel better about their own weaknesses.

Keeping your independence

You can get the most out of being part of a group or gang by keeping some independence. It is important to have several good relationships outside the group so that it does not become your whole world, and to leave it if your given role starts to make you feel uneasy or unhappy. It is also important to spend time alone.

Spending time away from your group of friends, and pursuing your own interests, gives you a balanced outlook.

Everybody else is doing it

The desire to fit in and earn your place as part of a gang, or to feel that you are getting as much out of life as other people of your age, is enormous. Young people put each other under a lot of pressure; to wear the latest fashions, to use 'in' words and phrases, and to be daring and fearless. This type of pressure is called **peer** pressure.

Where does peer pressure come from?

The **media**, advertisers and film-makers bombard us with images of how we should look and act. People naturally compare themselves with these glamorous ideals and usually feel they do not measure up. A large part of relating to our peers is based on comparing ourselves with them and comparing them with each other, to judge which of us comes closest to the glamorous ideals. We compete to be the most perfect amongst our peers, which may mean the most outrageous, the most stylish, or even the one who gets the best/worst results at school.

Do you ever feel peer pressure when you shop for clothes? It might lead you to buy an outfit that is very trendy but you know doesn't suit you.

When peer pressure is bad news

Wanting to stand out amongst peers can lead people to do things or behave in ways that they would not otherwise.

1. Committing crimes. This ranges from wrongdoing such as truanting from school, to painting graffiti, shoplifting or other forms of stealing.

CASE STUDY 1: THEFT

Josh started stealing more and bigger things because he thought it was the only thing about him that impressed his friends. They were all open-mouthed when he talked about being chased by the police through somebody's garden. Eventually, he got excluded from school. He ended up losing touch with his friends, and ruining his dream of future employment with a record company.

2. Making a bold statement with your appearance, that does not reflect your true personality.

CASE STUDY 2: TATTOOS

Sonia's best friend finally persuaded her to have a tattoo. Sonia chose the smallest she could and felt sick with fear about her mother seeing it. She had to spend all her savings from her Saturday job on a new dress in order to hide the tattoo at a family party, and six months later wanted to have it removed. She had not realized that removing it meant an expensive and painful operation, which involves taking skin from one part of the body to replace the patch of tattooed skin.

3. Taking risks with activities that could endanger your health. This includes smoking, drinking alcohol, taking drugs and having sex.

CASE STUDY 3: DRUGS

Danny and Safina both tried **ecstasy** at a party. Danny collapsed about four hours after taking the drug and had to be rushed to hospital. His body had **dehydrated** and he was lucky not to die. Safina spent the whole night after Danny had collapsed thinking that the same thing was going to happen to her and that her life was going to be over at the age of 14. She felt very alone, and was inconsolable until she knew the drug was safely out of her system.

Think about the consequences

People often lie about what they have said and done in order to impress their friends. They pretend, for example, to be far more sexually experienced than they are, or to have tried drugs that they have not, because they want to appear grown up. It is important not to be influenced by the boasting of others.

Think hard about what the consequences could be of everything you do, before you do it, and whether it is a risk worth taking and the right decision for you! Arm yourself with information by reading and looking up issues on the Internet.

FACT

32% (1/3) of boys between the ages of 8 and 15 said that their friends sometimes led them into trouble.

NSPCC *survey, 1996*

The new kid on the block

Meeting new people and making new friends is one of the most daunting and most exciting aspects of life. Your family situation might change, and bring with it a whole new group of people to get to know as 'family'; you may move school; you may want to take up a new hobby or sport and find other like-minded people to team up with.

All change

If you can get on with new people quickly, it will help you enormously throughout your life. Forty or fifty years ago, many people worked for the same company for their whole adult life, married in their early twenties and stayed married, and kept the same small group of friends until they died. These days, most people's lives are full of change, and changes in work and personal life mean meeting new people, some of whom may become friends.

We all want to be liked

Even the most self-confident people can feel awkward and self-conscious when they walk into a room where they don't know anybody. Whether you are new to a crowd that already knows each other, like on the first day at a new school when it is not the first year for everybody else, or you are part of a crowd with a new person in your midst, the most important thing to remember is that everybody wants to be liked. Also, people may look a lot more confident than they feel inside.

Look before you leap

When you meet someone new, it is a good idea not to attach yourself to them too firmly before you have had time to hang out, watch how they behave with other people and work out if they are your sort of person. Have you ever been in a situation where you have started spending all your free time with a new mate, only to realize a few weeks later that they got on your nerves? Of course, the opposite can also happen.

CASE STUDY

Jawara remembers avoiding Mick, who later became a good friend, for weeks when they were both new, because he thought Mick was avoiding his gaze every time he looked in his direction – it turned out that Mick could not see very far through his glasses!

FIVE WAYS TO MAKE NEW FRIENDS

- Compliment somebody on their clothes or haircut – it is the easiest way to start a conversation.

- Take up a new interest that you really enjoy – you could even start a group at school.

- Wear a t-shirt or bag with the name of your favourite bands, football club, or film stars – find a way to make it clear what your tastes are and like-minded people will find you.

- If you know more people than somebody else, approach the new person and invite them to join your group.

- Talk to somebody yourself to find out about them and decide whether you like them, rather than judge them according to other people's views.

When it all goes wrong

Relationships of all kinds can be as difficult as they are rewarding. Human beings change in their likes and wants, their lives change and they face new challenges that inevitably affect how they relate to others. For example, your easy-going friend may seem like a very different person if they are having a lot of family problems.

Healthy conflict

If you never argue with your friends, perhaps you should ask yourself if you feel that you can always be yourself with them and how honest you really are. We are all individuals, and it is normal and healthy to disagree with people we are close to and even to fall out from time to time.

Time to say goodbye?

Something may happen between you and a friend to make you want to end your friendship. This is bound to happen to some of your friendships, and only you can decide whether it is worth working to keep up a friendship which is difficult, or whether to let it go.

Most people hate conflict and try to avoid it, but some disagreement is inevitable and it shows that there is honesty within the friendship.

When people stop behaving like friends for no reason…

'Dear Agony Aunt
My mate Pete is always criticizing me in front of our other friends. If I get a spot he calls me "Pizza Face" loudly in the playground. I got a new mobile phone for my birthday, and he called me spoilt. We used to have a great laugh together, but he is just getting more and more vicious.'

This sounds like jealousy – the comment about the mobile phone is a sure sign that you've got something Pete wants. Something is making him feel bad about himself, so he is trying to make himself feel better by putting you down. Try to find out what might be bothering him underneath the bravado. Also, let him know that you will not put up with his insults, so he had better stop if he wants to stay friends.

When you fall out over something…

'Dear Agony Aunt
Me and my best mate fancied the same girl at school. I got one of her friends to tell her that my mate had a girlfriend who he had met on holiday. He found out somehow and was furious with me. I cannot see how we will ever be friends again. I have lost a friend and I did not even get the girl!'

Competition between friends can be healthy, but you lied and let your friend down badly. You need to apologize and try to convince him that you will never be so disloyal again. If you are good friends, this will hopefully blow over. If not, you will have learnt something important for future friendships.

When you grow apart…

'Dear Agony Aunt
My family moved house and I joined a new tennis club for the summer and got in with a fun new crowd. My friend, Shazia, used to hang out at my house all the time, but we just do not seem to have anything to say to each other anymore. She hates tennis, and we are not even at the same school now.'

Friendship is kept alive by sharing similar interests. It is important not to dump friends for new fads which may not last, but some friendships definitely have a shorter life span than others. It is natural to outgrow them and want to move on to people you have more in common with.

Can family be friends?

You can choose your friends, but you cannot choose your family. If family for you means a **foster family** or **care home**, most of this chapter still applies just as much to you.

Competition between brothers and sisters

Even if they are the same age as you, relationships with **siblings** can be very different from friendships outside of the family. The daily struggles to make friendships work can be multiplied several times when it comes to family relationships. There may be strong feelings of jealousy or envy.

Your relationship with your siblings might be your closest, but also your most difficult. They seldom let you get away with the things that your friends do, and you may experience strong feelings of envy towards them.

RELATIONSHIPS WITH YOUR FAMILY...

...can be your closest because:
- they know you better than anybody else does
- you can be totally yourself with them
- they put up with you, whatever mood you are in
- they stick by you, through good and bad times
- the older ones protect you and look after you
- you can argue with them and know that they will still be there afterwards
- they understand your personality because you have characteristics in common.

...can be the most difficult because:
- they tell you your faults bluntly and point out your bad behaviour
- they know how to wind you up
- they sometimes refuse to take your moods seriously
- they are the harshest teases, and sometimes make you look foolish in front of your friends
- they sometimes treat you like a young child
- you have the worst arguments with them
- you cannot just walk away if there are serious problems.

It may be because one sibling seems to be the parents' favourite, or is more talented at a certain activity, such as sport or art. An only child may feel lucky when he or she hears of how cruel siblings can be to each other. Unlike friends, siblings are unlikely to abandon you, so it is easy not to bother to try to treat them well. It is also human nature to take our frustrations out on the people we feel closest to.

Our immediate family home is where most of us first learn what we need to do to survive in the outside world, how to relate to other people, and how to stick up for ourselves. This learning starts in infancy, and, along with our parents, our siblings are the testing ground for exploring whether various ways of behaving are acceptable. For example many of us quickly learn that bullying is wrong through not being allowed to bully younger siblings. However this

> Do you have good memories of your older brother or sister helping you to learn something new when you were younger?

testing of extreme behaviour can make relationships between siblings very difficult at times.

Siblings can be your greatest friends

If you get on well with your brothers or sisters, they can provide a ready-made social life and a shoulder to cry on. Older siblings can be particularly helpful for talking through problems because they may well have experienced them themselves; you may feel able to talk to them about issues you do not want to talk to your parents about. If there are problems within the family, such as your parents quarrelling a lot, sharing the crisis will help to make you and your siblings feel less alone with it. As you get older the age gap between you, which may feel huge now, becomes meaningless and siblings often have close friendships as adults even if they fought constantly as children.

CASE STUDY

Sandra was two years below her sister in school, and found that teachers were always comparing her with Ruth. When Ruth became a prefect and captain of three sports teams in the sixth form, Sandra decided that she would go to the local sixth form college when the time came. This helped Sandra to feel less resentful towards Ruth, and led her to pursue her own interests in drama rather than feel like a failure because she was not naturally good at sport.

Take me seriously

> A charity called the National Children's Bureau trained five 16–17 year-olds to do research amongst 10–17 year-olds, to find out their views and concerns. 'Young Opinions, Great Ideas' was published in 1998, and this comment from one young person reflects the view of a lot of their peers:
>
> *They (adults) would say something like 'Yeah. Yeah, that's a good idea' and then move on to the next one or wouldn't take it into consideration. And they would be surprised that we've got our own ideas. When we say we want this, they go, 'No you don't, you want this', and they go and like just tell us what we want.*

Young people often feel frustrated and powerless in the company of adults. How can you have any sort of friendship with give and take when one of you, that is the adult, has all the advantages?

Equality

Friendship between **peers** is usually based on **equality**. Adults and young people can easily feel dismissed by each other because of the differences in their age, life experience and worldly power. Although it is important that adults show young teenagers **respect**, it is wrong for adults to treat them as adults in every way, because they are some years away from taking full responsibility for themselves. However, some feelings of equality can still be established through give and take in everyday discussions, for example.

Respect

To build a good relationship, both adult and young person must clearly show in words and actions that they recognize that they are not equal, but have respect for the other because of their qualities as an individual person, regardless of age. A young person cannot be friends with an adult unless they feel that they are taken seriously by them. Teenagers may find it easier to talk about their problems with a friend's mother rather than their own, for example, because their friend's mother does not treat them like a child.

65 YEARS AGE DIFFERENCE!

One sixth form project in England has shown that age difference does not have to be a barrier to friendship. A young **volunteer** is paired up with an older person who lives near their school, and who has a problem with sight. The volunteer visits the older person every week, reads their post and does other tasks for them. Reading somebody's post is very personal and requires trust in the volunteer, and a close relationship can develop where both parties learn from each other's experience. One volunteer who wants to study law at university is visiting a retired judge, for example.

Older people may have more to offer you than you think. This sixth-former volunteers to visit an older person, who in turn is helping him to prepare for the career he wants to follow.

Variety in friendship

A relationship with an older person can give you a different kind of friendship from your peers. Some young people have a mentor, for example. This is an older person who helps them by giving guidance on an aspect of their life such as their school work, or a hobby or sport. If you do not have close family relationships with older people, or perhaps do not have a father or mother, a mentor could be especially helpful. Some adults have mentors, who might be people who are higher up in the same profession as themselves, who help them to avoid repeating common mistakes and to make the most of their potential.

Be aware of the risks

Friendships with adults can be exciting and rewarding, but there can be risks in making friends with somebody much older than yourself. There are some adults who make friends with children and teenagers because they find it difficult to make friends with their own peers. Others enjoy feeling that they can have influence or some control over the younger person because they are in a more powerful position. There is a small minority of adults who it may be dangerous to become friends with because they see young people as an opportunity to be **abusive**.

If an adult starts saying or doing things that make you feel uncomfortable, it is best to avoid being on your own with them, and to stop seeing them altogether if the situation continues. If you are worried by an adult's treatment of you, find another adult who you trust and talk it through with them.

Teacher's pet?

Your relationships with your teachers are based on both of you having a clear **role** – they teach and you learn. You have no choice in this part of the relationship, and the relationship is most successful if you can **respect** the **authority** they have because of their role, in the same way that you respect your parents' authority.

You will have different relationships with each of your teachers, depending on whether you like and trust them, whether you think they teach well, and whether you feel that they take you seriously. You may feel singled out by one as 'teacher's pet', and ignored by another.

If you have a personal problem and need to talk to an adult outside of your family, a teacher that you like may be the ideal person. They will make time for you if you need it.

Help with problems

A teacher who you get on well with and respect is the best person to talk through problems relating to your work, or other problems such as bullying at school. If you have a serious problem that has nothing to do with school, but is distressing you, such as family problems or a problem with drugs, a teacher may be the best starting point for helping you to sort it out.

Teachers have many pressures on their time. This means that it is important to approach them for help in the right way and at the right time. Trying to tell them about something personal in a public corridor between lessons is a bad idea, for example. The best thing to do is to ask them when they can put some time aside to talk to you somewhere quiet. This will ensure that they can give you their undivided attention, and you are more likely to feel listened to and to get the help you want. They may advise you on somebody else to talk to who knows more about your problem issue than they do, or they may be able to help you directly.

Crushes

If you talk to your parents and other adults you know, many of them will remember having crushes on their favourite teachers at school. You may have one teacher who always seems to know about everything, and who makes lessons especially interesting. Maybe you admire the way they dress, or their voice, for example. Before you know it, you

have started to think of them as a perfect hero or heroine. You think about them constantly and have very strong feelings for them. You may even feel **sexual attraction** towards them.

Crushes happen when we build somebody up in our minds and forget that they are an ordinary human being, with their fair share of problems and weaknesses. Often we do not even realize that this is what we are doing. As well as teachers, it is very common to have a crush on a film or pop star, or sporting hero or heroine. How many posters do you have in your bedroom of people you admire? Have you got a crush on any of them?

Crushes can feel confusing, but they normally pass or your attention moves to a new person. The fastest way to get over a crush is not to allow it to rule your life. Keep enjoying your friends and interests, and try to resist the temptation to daydream about your crush so much that it affects your school work and the chance of having fun.

Crushes are a natural part of growing up, but the feelings can be very powerful. The more real relationships you have in your life, the less likely you are to be taken over by a crush.

Who am I?

We have started to explore some of the different types of relationships you have with other people, and what is needed to build good relationships with others. But what kind of relationship do you have with yourself? How well do you think you know and understand yourself? How much do you accept yourself without criticizing yourself in your own head or to other people? Do you like yourself? And how does your attitude towards yourself affect your relationships with others?

Do you feel good about yourself most of the time? It is easier to feel good about other people if you do.

Self-esteem

Think about the people you feel closest to. Think how much you love and **respect** them. Do you have the same warm feelings when you think about yourself as a person? A lot of people of all ages are much harsher in their judgement of themselves than of other people, and do not value themselves as highly as they value others. If a friend gets a low grade in an exam, for example, it will not affect their good opinion of that friend as a person, but if they do badly themselves they may tell themselves harshly: 'I am a failure'.

Research shows that people who have high **self-esteem** are most likely to be successful in every aspect of their lives. **Psychiatrists** say that it is not possible to fully love other people unless we love ourselves.

Self-esteem has been shown to have a bigger effect on how well people do at school and university than their level of intelligence does. Does that surprise you? High self-esteem does not mean thinking that you are perfect and can do no wrong. It means valuing yourself and being kind to yourself, whatever situation you may find yourself in. It means forgiving yourself if you do or say things that you feel are wrong, and being able to forget your mistakes rather than dwelling on them.

People with high self-esteem spend more time thinking about their successes than their failures, and believe that they are basically worthwhile people. Unlike people with a low opinion of themselves, they do not have to put other people down, or bully them, or try to gain power over them, in order to feel better about themselves. Low self-esteem is sadly a very big problem amongst people of all ages. How many people do you know who you think really like themselves most of the time?

Know yourself

In order to learn to make the most of life and to take the right decisions for yourself as you grow up, you need to know your likes and dislikes, what makes you feel fulfilled and contented, what interests you, and what kind of relationships you want. Do you enjoy socializing in a large crowd, or do you prefer to spend your spare time with one or two close friends, for example? Everybody is different, and some people need more **personal space** than others. Most people prefer to divide their spare time into time spent alone, especially if they have important changes in their lives to think through, and time spent having fun and relaxing with family or friends.

FACTS

- *42% of 8–15 year-olds say they don't like being on their own but prefer to be with friends.*
- *55% say they don't mind being on their own, but like to be with their friends some of the time.*
- *3% say they usually like to be on their own.*

NSPCC *survey, 1996*

Right and wrong

Most children are taught the basic differences between right and wrong from a young age. As they grow up and become independent individuals, they learn to think for themselves about important and complicated issues such as whether it is ever acceptable to tell a lie. Their opinions about issues like these are one of the main things that make them an individual. What opinions do you hold that you think make you the person you are, and make you different from some people who you know?

27

All alone

However many good relationships we have, we all have times when we feel all alone in the world and full of sadness and despair. These feelings are a normal and healthy reaction to major disappointment or an event such as somebody close to us being very unhappy, or ill, or dying. It is also normal to have some days when we have these feelings seemingly for no reason. An American **psychiatrist**, Dr David Burns, says that the average person feels basically happy (meaning contented and positive) five days out of seven in a week. By the average person, Dr Burns means those of us without serious problems, and who are free of traumas such as war, being a refugee, or living in poverty.

You can change your mood

We all know people who seem to be able to sail through life with a smile most of the time, and others who always look worried and sad. Psychiatrists say that it is not what happens to you, it is how you react that is most important.

From time to time, it is natural to be sad and feel that nobody could really understand what we are feeling.

Positive thinking

The mind is very powerful, and our thoughts and feelings are closely linked. If you are feeling miserable, counting your blessings may sound like a cliché, but it works. Write down three good things that have happened to you in the past week. However you were feeling before, you are undoubtedly feeling even better now.

THINK POSITIVE

When we are feeling low, we usually see things in the worst light. Try thinking positively instead.

✘ Negative thinking: 'I'm never going to get this school project finished in time.'

✔ Positive thinking: 'I'll take it one step at a time and do as well as I can.'

✘ Negative: 'Why did Nas ignore me this morning? What have I done?'

✔ Positive: 'Is Nas okay? Has anything happened over the weekend to make him distracted.'

Looking after yourself

When life looks bleak, it is important to keep in good health. Research has shown that being deprived of sleep can actually cause people to become depressed. Exercise is also particularly helpful, because the activity releases natural chemicals into the body which give a feeling of wellbeing. Eating healthily and drinking plenty of water will also help you to cope better. Talking about how you feel to other people you trust is important during difficult times.

Suicide

Sometimes people become so wrapped up in feelings of despair and hopelessness that they can no longer see any point in living. Their **self-esteem** may be so low that they feel they are a burden to the people they have the closest relationships with – their family and friends. Every year, around 2000 young people talk to the helpline Childline about feeling **suicidal**.

SIGNS THAT YOU MIGHT BE SERIOUSLY DEPRESSED

Depression can become an illness. If you have experienced any of the following for a period of several weeks or months, you should talk to a responsible adult about getting help:

● I feel like a failure and don't feel positive about anything in my life.

● I always feel tired and don't seem to have any energy.

● I am eating far more/less than usual.

● I sleep very badly and wake up very early in the morning.

● I think about death and things that upset me a lot.

● Even small things make me snappy and irritable.

FACTS

● *18% of 13–17 year-olds felt they had nobody to talk to.*
● *over 42% felt at times there was no point in living.*
● *over 11% had tried to commit suicide.*

Survey by the Samaritans charity, 1996

The bigger picture

The kind of relationship you have with yourself and with other people is influenced by other aspects of your life. Do you sometimes see your relationships as your whole world, or are you always aware of how they fit into the 'bigger picture'? Examples of a 'bigger picture' might be your religious beliefs, or what a healthy **society** means to you and what you do to help, for example getting involved in a local environmental project.

These people's relationships fit into their 'bigger picture' of the kind of society they enjoy being part of. They share an interest in taking part in events on behalf of a good cause – a cause they believe is important. How do your friends fit with the other things which mean a lot to you?

Strong beliefs

Some people have strong beliefs, either connected to a particular religion or **philosophy**. When they experience distressing events, they find comfort in their beliefs and use them to make sense of what has happened and to come to terms with it. When good things happen to them, they celebrate in the same way.

People with strong beliefs often form their strongest relationships with others who share the same beliefs, and may find it hard to treat people who do not share their beliefs with **equality**. You may experience great difficulty in your relationship with your parents and other members of your family if they have strong beliefs which you decide that you do not share when you grow up.

Cultural background

Do you have a large family with lots of cousins who you spend time with regularly? Does your family always eat a meal together in the evening? Is your home life noisy or normally peaceful? Many people do not even realize that all families have different routines until they spend time in somebody else's home! Having friends who have been brought up with a different cultural background to your own teaches you that there are almost as many different ways of living as there are people. It is easy to believe that 'there is only one way to do things', but discovering new ways can make life more interesting and rewarding.

Living in a healthy society

People need to be able to live alongside complete strangers as well as the people they know and love, and to act for the best for everybody rather than behave selfishly, in order to have a healthy society. What kind of relationship do you have with your environment, for example? Do you throw litter into the street? Do you travel by car when you could just as easily walk and save valuable resources while avoiding polluting the air with exhaust fumes? Do you take your responsibilities as a **citizen** seriously? There are lots of opportunities to **volunteer** some of your spare time to help charities whose work you value, or to support individuals who may be less fortunate than you. This is also an excellent way to meet new people, widen your circle of friends and develop new interests.

RACISM

Racism is one of many kinds of prejudice that people can hold about other people. Do you hold prejudices? The word 'prejudice' literally means 'pre-judge', and means that you are making up your mind about what a person is like, and what they stand for, before you have enough information about them to be able to do that properly. Prejudice is one of the biggest barriers to having a fulfilling variety of friendships.

It is a sad fact that you will encounter racist attitudes in many aspects of life. Some people, and maybe your own family, might disapprove if you become friends with somebody from a different racial background. **Racism** can put a lot of strain on a relationship, but it is important to explain to people with a negative attitude that you **respect** your friend because of their character, and that their skin colour, background and so on does not make them better or worse than anybody else.

Time for romance

The teenage years are the time when you start to explore new kinds of relationships.

Sexual attraction

The physical changes in your body during **puberty** also produce changes in how you respond to other people. You may start to feel attracted to people you know already, or whom you meet for the first time, in a new and different way. These feelings are different from friendship because they involve sexual feelings. You want to be physically near to the other person, to kiss them and to touch them. Holding somebody's hand suddenly becomes an activity that fills you with warm, pleasurable feelings. You may get butterflies in your stomach immediately you see the person or hear their voice.

Why do we feel sexually attracted to some people and not to others? Nobody has a full answer, and scientists have done a great deal of research to try to solve the mystery. This aspect of life is different for everybody. Some people are sexually attracted to a wide variety of types of people, while others may only ever fancy one type. Some people find themselves attracted to several different people at any one time, while others focus on one person.

Feeling sexually attracted to somebody is an exciting and sometimes almost overwhelming experience. Have you ever felt 'swept off your feet' by somebody else?

Getting obsessed

You may feel overwhelmed at times by how strong your **emotions** are. You may want to spend most of your time with a special boyfriend or girlfriend. It is normal to go through a stage when you find it hard not to spend all your time thinking about the other person if you are not with them.

This becomes unhealthy if you start to change your natural behaviour because you are concentrating so much on wanting to please somebody else. It is easy to forget that being yourself was good enough to attract the other person in the first instance, and you may find yourself claiming that you like the things that they like, such as a particular band, or smoking, when really you don't. This sort of behaviour is caused by feeling insecure about the extent to which they like you compared to the amount you like them, and wanting to make them like you more. It is hard work to keep up the pretence of being somebody you are not

for long, and it is unlikely to make them feel more keen on you anyway.

Obsession can lead to allowing somebody else to influence you to do things you know are wrong for you, rather like **peer** pressure, because keeping them attracted to you feels more important than standing up for what you believe in (see Min's letter on page 38).

Romance is fun

Dealing with new feelings can be daunting, and may make you feel as if you no longer have full control over yourself. But **sexual attraction** becomes a normal part of life as you become an adult, and romance can be one of life's greatest pleasures. Sitting beside the person you fancy in the cinema makes watching a film a far more enjoyable experience, and knowing that somebody else fancies you can make your **self-esteem** soar! Romance is also the starting point of developing important long-term relationships.

Do I fancy her or him?

Sexuality

Human beings are all different in terms of their sexual desires and who they feel sexually attracted to, just as they are different in other aspects of their lives.

Trying to work out what your true feelings are for somebody else can be a very confusing experience, especially at the stage when you are learning about new kinds of relationships.

Homosexuality

The majority of people are sexually attracted to people of the opposite sex, but many millions of people throughout the world are sexually attracted to people of the same sex. They are **homosexual**, or **gay**; women who are gay are also referred to as lesbians. Some people fancy people of both sexes – they are known as bisexual.

Confusion is normal

When you are experiencing new feelings and relationships, it is normal to be very confused at times about how you really do feel about different people. You may not know whether you are attracted to girls, boys, neither or both. You do not have to make a decision. This is a time in your life for exploring your feelings. What is important is to try not to do anything that you might regret in later life, and to try not to hurt other people's or your own feelings while you learn what **sexual attraction** means for you.

Clouding your mind and feelings by taking drugs and alcohol tends to add to confusion. It can be tempting to use them to dull feelings of awkwardness or shyness, but you may well know people who have behaved in ways they later regret because they were under the influence of drugs or alcohol. Wild parties can be great fun and create a relaxed environment for talking or dancing with people you might find sexually attractive. But it is worth remembering that you will have to face all these people again and behave accordingly. Is there an occasion you look back on and feel red-faced about? What would you do differently another time?

Talk it over

Many teenagers find it useful to talk to somebody older, who they trust, to help them to work through their thoughts and feelings. There are organizations and individual counsellors who spend all day every day talking to young people about their concerns around sexual attraction. If you think that you might be gay, it is important to talk to somebody who is able to listen without judging you, or trying to persuade you either towards or away from homosexuality.

Homophobia

This word literally means 'fear of homosexuality', and describes an attitude that is held by many people and many cultures throughout the world. There are numerous demeaning slang words for homosexuals in every language. Sexuality is a very personal matter – imagine how you would feel if you discovered that other people disliked you just because you had homosexual feelings? Gay people continue to campaign to be treated the same as **heterosexuals** by society.

So many people behave in ways and say things that suggest that anybody who is gay is a freak, that it can make young people fearful that they might turn out to be gay. The truth is that gay people are just as likely to lead happy and fulfilled lives as heterosexuals. The most unhappy people are people who remain confused about sexual attraction throughout their adulthood, and are not able to have successful romantic relationships at all.

Playing games

Sexual attraction can make you feel so different from usual that you say and do things that make you cringe when you think about them later. It is easy to resent the person who is making your stomach churn every time you see them, and find yourself treating them badly. At times like this it is best to try to think how you would treat them if they were any other of your friends. Also, how would you like to be treated by them?

Power play

If you know that somebody is attracted to you, it can make you feel very powerful. Immature people get **abusive** and play games with the other person's feelings, like a cat might play with its prey. Confident people do not need to mess other people around (putting them down in front of their friends, for example) in order to boost their own self-confidence.

Dealing with rejection

Feeling sexually attracted to somebody can be a painful experience if they do not feel the same way about you, or if their feelings change when you get to know each other better. Although it may seem as though they are controlling your feelings, you can 'let go' of them and the painful way you feel if you try to concentrate on other things and distract yourself.

Romance can be painful. Can you imagine how this girl might be feeling, seeing the person she fancies with somebody else?

YOU ARE MOST LIKELY TO ENJOY SUCCESS IN ROMANCE IF:

- You make a bit of an effort with your appearance for a date and make sure you arrive promptly.

  This shows that the occasion is important to you. The other person will feel cared for and respected. And you'll be feeling your best too.

- You make an effort to get to know somebody else by listening properly and finding out what is important to them.

  This shows that you are genuinely interested in them and is vital for a good relationship to grow. They will feel valued and be more likely to want to listen to you in return.

- You take it in turns to choose how you spend your time together, and introduce each other to the things that you each enjoy.

  *This is **equality**, and keeps the relationship alive and exciting through new experiences. Boredom can set in very easily in romance!*

- You communicate honestly with the other person. You tell them how you feel, and share your problems and successes with them.

  They will be more likely to be honest with you, and you will both feel more secure in your friendship.

YOU NEED TO GET YOUR ACT TOGETHER IF:

- You stand somebody up for a date. In other words, you arrange to meet somebody and don't bother to turn up or to let them know that you are not coming.

  *This is cowardly and **disrespectful** of somebody else's time and feelings. They will feel foolish and angry. Think how you would feel.*

- You talk about yourself in an effort to impress somebody else, and hardly let them get a word in.

  This is rude, and usually happens because you feel unconfident. The other person will feel unimportant and angry.

- You make all the decisions about how you spend your time together.

  This is selfish. The other person will feel bossed around and assume you do not care about their interests.

- You hide your feelings and try to act cool at all times.

  This is foolish if you do want to have a good relationship. The other person will feel confused and probably get bored with going out with a 'brick wall' very quickly.

Hard to say no?

Feeling attracted to somebody else in a sexual way means that you are having all the normal physical and **emotional** responses for somebody of your age. Research shows that young teenagers are not yet ready for a full, adult **sexual relationship**, because they are not yet fully mature either physically or emotionally. It is illegal in the UK to have sex under the age of 16.

Sex and reality

A sexual relationship involves strong feelings, and should be taken very seriously. We constantly see stories and clips on television and in films which focus on the exciting and fun aspects of sex. These aspects are important, and can make it hard to resist experimenting with sex. But having sex at the wrong time or with the wrong person can lead to regrets and serious problems, such as an unwanted pregnancy or a **sexually transmitted infection**.

Different attitudes to sex

Many religions and cultures say that it is wrong to have sex outside of marriage. Everybody is different, and has their own moral beliefs about the rights and wrongs of sex. There are people who go through life having lots of brief relationships, but most people enjoy sex best as part of a strong **committed relationship**. What are your beliefs about the rights and wrongs of having sex?

Feeling pressured into sex...

'Dear Agony Aunt
I was in my boyfriend's bedroom recently and we were kissing. He got pushy with me and started touching me in a way I was not ready for. I really like him and I was too scared to stop him in case he didn't want to see me again or told our friends that I was cold and immature. Now I feel I let him go too far, but I don't want to lose him. What should I do?'
Min (age 13)

Do you think he knew that you felt uncomfortable about him touching you like that? Communication is the key to both of you feeling positive in your relationship, and you won't feel relaxed with him again unless you tell him that you want to stop at kissing. Then you will both know where you stand and you can enjoy getting to know each other without either of you feeling pressurized. Lots of boys and girls feel that they have to take a sexual relationship as far as the other person will let them – mainly because of peer pressure – and may be secretly relieved to be stopped by the other person. It is a good idea to avoid situations such as being alone in your boyfriend's bedroom in the future.

People often don't speak up because of fear, but what do you really need to be scared of in standing up for what you want around the issue of sex? If a boy or girl is only interested in you for sex, or is the kind of person who would put you down in front of your friends, is this somebody you even want to kiss?

FACTS

- *The majority of young people under the age of 17 have not had sex.*
- *Some sexually transmitted infections cannot be cured, and may lead to an inability to have children.*
- *Almost 50% (1/2) of all **conceptions** in the UK, and 1 in 3 births, are unplanned.*
- *75% of women who have a pregnancy terminated knew about emergency **contraception**, but failed to obtain it.*
- *The UK has the highest rate of pregnancy amongst teenagers of all western European countries.*

Most people find that it is more satisfying to form a good friendship with somebody before they experiment with sex. If somebody is already a friend, a level of trust has been formed which makes talking about the sexual side of the relationship easier. It also means that the relationship is more likely to last for a while, since you already know whether you really do like each other or not.

Having sex may feel like harmless experimentation, but the reality is very different for thousands of young women across the UK every year. Being a parent before you are ready can take away your own youth and prevent you from doing the things in life that you most want to do.

Just the two of us

Putting on blinkers

When you feel attracted to somebody, and they feel the same way, it is easy to act like a horse wearing blinkers – you forget the world around you and can only see in one direction! Spending time with each other feels so exciting that everyday life, and the people in it, seem dull in comparison.

But as they say, you can have too much of a good thing, and spending all your time with one person is certainly the fastest way to get bored with them. If you introduce them into your everyday life, in the same way you would introduce any new friend, you will get a much better idea of what they are like as a person and how well the two of you get on. You can learn a lot by meeting their friends and family too.

Do not abandon your friends

This is the age when you are experimenting with starting romantic relationships, and during this period you may have several romances as you learn about **sexual attraction**. Your other friends are especially valuable now, to talk over problems with and to help you keep your feet on the ground as you experience strong feelings. They are also there as a shoulder to cry on if your romance goes wrong, and to get you out having fun again instead of wallowing in misery. Romance is only one part of a full life. Besides, a person with lots of friends and interests is much more attractive than one with few or none.

In the film *Grease*, Danny feels torn between hanging out with his cool group of friends, and pursuing Sandy, who he met on holiday. It takes him the whole duration of the film to get the balance right!

I started going out with a girl and was completely smitten. I started avoiding my gang in the evenings to hang out with her. She's dumped me now, and the gang hasn't exactly welcomed me back with open arms.

What do you think the problem is?

Sparky as good as told his mates that they were unimportant, so their behaviour is understandable. It is foolish to abandon friends for the sake of romance. Sparky will probably have lots of different girlfriends over the next few years, but his friends are more likely to be around for a long time.

When I'm alone with my girlfriend, things are great between us. She is like a different person if her friends are there, and ignores me. I feel left out and awkward.

What do you think the problem is?

Peer pressure can make people self-conscious; she probably doesn't want her friends to know that she's bothered about Wayne in case they tease her. Do you remember how Danny behaved in the film *Grease*?

I had a row with Stef because he wanted to spend Saturday night playing with his computer instead of seeing me. I decided that he obviously didn't care about me.

What do you think the problem is?

If he always put his computer first, then Jenny might have jumped to the right conclusion. But everybody needs time to themselves, however much they care about other people.

Getting the balance right

It is important to find a good balance between spending time with your friends, time with somebody you want to get to know in a romantic way, and time on your own. You will probably feel too self-conscious to have good communication with somebody you are sexually attracted to in front of your friends, especially when you are trying to find out whether they feel the same way about you, so time spent alone together is important.

Dear John

A 'Dear John' letter is a slang term for a letter telling somebody that you want to end your romantic relationship with them. You may start to go out with somebody and then realize that you don't get on as well with them as you thought you would. Whatever the reason, it is up to you who you socialize with, and it is not wrong to end a romantic relationship if you want to. But it is important to communicate clearly with the other person and to try not to be unnecessarily hurtful. Write them a 'Dear John' letter if that is the bravest you can be, but it is best to talk to them face to face if you can.

CASE STUDY 1

Tim suddenly started to behave strangely towards his girlfriend. He made excuses about feeling too tired to see her, but insisted that he wanted to go out the following week. He never telephoned her again, and did not return her telephone calls. How do you think she felt? Would it not have been better if Tim had been brave enough to tell her the truth?

CASE STUDY 2

This is what Salim did in a similar situation…
Salim wanted to end a romance. He felt guilty. He knew his girlfriend would feel hurt and he also felt nervous about her getting angry with him. But he wanted to treat her with **respect**, so he arranged to meet her for coffee and explained briefly how he felt. He also told her how much he had enjoyed the fun they had shared over the past few weeks. How do you think she felt?

Salim behaved bravely, allowed his girlfriend to express how she felt if she wanted to, and turned the time they had spent together into the basis for a new friendship. Tim let himself down, which was bad for his own **self-esteem**, and left his girlfriend feeling confused and wary of trusting boys to do what they said they would in the future. She felt she had been treated as if she did not exist and that the weeks of fun they had shared had been made meaningless by his cowardly behaviour at the end.

Endings are painful

When romance ends it can feel very painful. You may experience strong feelings of loss that are similar to the feelings of loss you have if you move house and leave friends behind. You can even experience milder but similar grief to that felt by people when somebody close to them dies.

Apart from feeling sad, you may also find it difficult to accept what has happened, feel angry towards whoever or whatever has caused your pain, and be fearful of forming new relationships because you are afraid of feeling this way again. You may have physical reactions such as a churning in your stomach, a change in appetite, or feelings of tiredness.

Moving forward

Whatever has ended in your life, looking after yourself will help you to recover a positive outlook. It is important to take time and **personal space** to work through your many thoughts and feelings about what has happened. Talking to other people you trust can help enormously, even though you may find it difficult to admit how you are feeling to somebody else.

Endings are a difficult aspect of life, but it is important to remember that you learn and grow through experiences like having relationships. However bad you feel at one time because something important to you has ended, there will always be an exciting new beginning of some kind just around the corner.

When something you were enjoying comes to an end, or somebody leaves you, it can feel like the end of the world. However, endings are an important part of new beginnings.

Glossary

abusive treating badly or taking unfair advantage

acquaintance somebody you know a little, but not well enough to call a friend

authority power to give orders, usually by having a formal role or duty

body language physical gestures which reveal important clues about how somebody is feeling; running fingers through hair repeatedly can be a sign of nervousness, for example

care home an alternative home to living with a family, usually run by the council. A carer is the person who plays the role of parent

citizen somebody who lives in a nation or state, living by the laws of the government and having certain rights and duties

committed relationship a relationship which both people regard as serious and long-term

conception fertilization of the female egg by the male sperm, marking the beginning of a pregnancy

confidential keeping something to yourself

contraception methods of preventing pregnancy, such as condoms

counsellor somebody who is trained in helping people with problems that involve deep feelings

dehydrated excessive loss of water from the body's tissues

disrespectful to treat someone without consideration

ecstasy an illegal drug, also known as 'e', which causes the body to dehydrate (lose water)

emotions feelings

equality having equal value and importance, regardless of differences

foster family family which is not related to a child, but brings the child up

gay sexually attracted to people of the same gender

heterosexual somebody who is sexually attracted to people of the opposite gender

homosexual somebody who is sexually attracted to people of the same gender

media the organizations which communicate news, such as television, radio, newspapers and magazines

peers people of the same age as you, for example in your class at school

personal space privacy and distance from other people

perspective to put into proper proportion

philosophy a system of meaning to make sense of what happens in life and the world

professional someone who is specially trained to do a job

psychiatrist doctor of the mind rather than the body

puberty the period when a child's body is developing into that of an adult

racism treating somebody differently because of their racial background

respect to value someone and treat them with consideration

role part played by a person in life or in an event or performance such as a play

self-esteem estimation of self-worth

sexual or physical abuse treating someone badly using sexual means or physical power to take advantage of them

sexual attraction having sexual feelings towards another person

sexually transmitted infections (STIs) diseases spread between partners during sex

sexual relationship relationship which involves having sex

siblings brothers and sisters

society everyone who is living by agreed rules shaped by the government – a healthy society is one where everybody contributes to helping people live and work together well

sociable enjoying the company of other people

suicidal likely to commit suicide (that is, to take one's own life)

volunteer person who gives their time of their own free will and without payment

Contacts and helplines

BROOKS ADVISORY CENTRES
020 7713 9000 – Advice on pregnancy and contraception

CHILDLINE
Freepost 1111, London, N1 0BR
0800 400 222 – 24-hour helpline. Children can phone or write with a problem of any kind

CRE (THE COMMISSION FOR RACIAL EQUALITY)
Elliott House, 10–12 Allington Street, London SW1E 5EH 020 7828 7022; Edinburgh 0131 226 5186; Cardiff 029 2038 8977 – Works to stop racist behaviour

CRUSE (Bereavement Care)
126 Sheen Road, Richmond, Surrey TW9 1UR. Helpline 020 8332 7227 (9.30–5pm Mon–Fri)

THE EATING DISORDERS ASSOCIATION
02603 621414 – Advice on eating disorders

FAMILY PLANNING CENTRES
020 7837 4044 – Advice on pregnancy and contraception

KIDSCAPE
152 Buckingham Palace Road, London SW1 9TR 020 7730 3300 – Gives advice on keeping safe, bullying etc. Send large stamped addressed envelope for information pack

LESBIAN AND GAY SWITCHBOARD
01712 837 7324 – Advice on homosexuality

NATIONAL DRUGS HELPLINE
0800 776600 – Advice on drug problems

THE NATIONAL CHILDREN'S BUREAU
8 Wakely Street, London EC1V 7QE
020 7843 6000 – www.ncb.org.uk
Works to identify and promote the well-being and interests of all children across every aspect of their lives

NSPCC (National Society for the Prevention of Cruelty to Children)
National Centre, 42 Curtain Road, London EC2A 3NH 020 7825 2500
Child Protection Helpline: 0800 800 500

SAMARITANS
0345 909090 – 24-hour helpline for anybody with a problem of any kind

SAVE THE CHILDREN
17 Grove Lane, London SE5 8RD
020 7703 5400 – Works for a fairer world for children

WWW.VOIS.ORG.UK
a web site with links to individual charities and advice on volunteering

YOUTH2YOUTH
020 8896 3675
www.youth2youth.co.uk
e-mail: help@youth2youth.co.uk – Helpline for young people run by young people

YOUNG MINDS
102–108 Clerkenwell Road, London EC1M 5SA
www.youngminds.org.uk – Information on mental health issues and young people

IN AUSTRALIA

ALCOHOL AND DRUGS TELEPHONE COUNSELLING & INFORMATION
1800 136 385, 03 9416 1818

CHILD PROTECTION SERVICE
13 1278

KIDS HELPLINE
1800 551800 – Free for advice and support

REACH OUT
www.reachout.asn.au – Helps children with a variety of problems

SAVE THE CHILDREN, AUSTRALIA
66 Sackfield Street, Collingwood, VIC 3066
03 94 16 0499

YOUTH, FAMILY & COMMUNITY SERVICES
03 9616 7300

Further reading

Fiction

Aquila
Andrew Norriss
Puffin, 1997

Are you there God, it's me Margaret
Judy Blume
Macmillan Children's Books, 1994

Forever
Judy Blume
Macmillan Children's Books, 1995

Memories of Anne Frank: Reflections of a Childhood Friend
Alison Leslie Gold
Scholastic, 1997

The Secret Garden
Frances Hodgson Burnett
Penguin Popular Classics, 1995
(First published in 1911)

Skellig
David Almond
Signature, 1998

The Tulip Touch
Anne Fine
Puffin, 1997

Non-fiction

Adolescence
Nicholas Tucker
Wayland Press,
Human Development Series, 1990

Child Abuse
Angela Park
Franklin Watts, 1998

Contemporary Moral Issues
Joe Jenkins
Heinemann, 1998

Divorce
Liz Friedrich
Franklin Watts, 1988

Marriage and Divorce
Separation and Divorce
Craig Donnellan
Independence, *Issues for the Nineties* Series, 1996

Rights in the Home
E Haughton and P Clarke
Franklin Watts, 1997

Young Opinions, Great Ideas – views of 70 young people aged 10–17 years throughout England on their concerns and views on life. Survey from the National Children's Bureau, 1998

Index